Take the

holy

moments

CHALLENGE

21 Days that Will Change Your Life

HolyMomentsChallenge.com

Imagine how many *holy* moments you will set in motion by introducing this idea to six people!

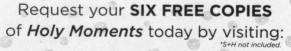

Request your **SIX FREE COPIES** of *Holy Moments* today by visiting:
S+H not included.

HolyMomentsBook.com

Offer available only in the U.S.

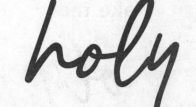

holy
moments

A Handbook for the Rest of Your Life

Matthew Kelly

BLUE
sparrow

Copyright © 2022
Kakadu, LLC
Published by Blue Sparrow
An Imprint of Viident

To learn more about the author, visit:
MatthewKelly.com

To learn more about the Holy Moments Movement, visit:
HolyMoments.Info

ISBN: 978-1-63582-135-2 (hardcover)
ISBN: 978-1-63582-136-9 (eBook)

Design by Ashley Dias

10   9   8   7   6   5

FIRST EDITION

Printed in the United States of America

table of contents

PART THREE: THE DIVINE PLAN

PART FOUR: THE POWER OF ONE IDEA

prologue

ONCE UPON A TIME there was a monastery deep in the forest. It was full of monks, they were full of joy, that joy was contagious, and people traveled from far and wide to visit.

One day a young man asked the Abbot why people came to the monastery. "Most come looking for answers to their questions," the old monk explained. The young man was curious what type of questions people asked. The Abbot continued, "They come seeking answers to the same questions all men and women ponder. What should I do with my life? Am I wasting my one short life? Where do I find meaning? How do I get the most out of life?"

The young man had traveled a long distance to visit the monastery, and as he walked away the old monk wondered what question the young man's heart was wrestling with.

Time passed and life at the monastery changed. It was ever so gradual at first. A couple of the monks became cranky. They had slowly closed their hearts to God and each other. Other monks became jealous. A younger monk was more handsome and popular with the visitors. Some of the monks began to argue about things of no consequence, and the poison of gossip crept into the monastery.

Visitors noticed that little by little life at the monastery was deteriorating. They perceived the monks were losing their joy, they noticed the monks were not as kind to each other, and over time they observed the monks growing impatient with their visitors.

The seasons came and went, and fewer visitors came to the monastery, until one day, the people stopped coming altogether.

The Abbot rose each morning an hour before his

brother monks and sat in the chapel asking God to give him the wisdom necessary to revitalize the monastery. But another summer came and went, and in the depths of the coldest winter ever, a profound sadness gripped the old Abbot's heart. He thought he had tried everything.

For hundreds of years people had come here longing for a glimpse of God and the monastery had thrived. What had he done wrong? He was wrapped with guilt and shame. The gap between his faith and his life had widened, and he didn't know how to close it.

On the first day of spring, the Abbot announced at breakfast that he was leaving the monastery to make a journey.

"Where are you going?" Brother Killian asked.

"I will visit the Hermit in the mountains to seek his counsel on our situation here at the monastery."

There was a wise Hermit who lived in the mountains thirty miles to the north. People traveled into the mountains to seek his wisdom. The Hermit and the Abbot had been childhood friends, but this the other monks did not know.

"When will you return?" Brother Owen asked.

"Three days," the Abbot replied.

"Who is in charge while you are gone?" Brother Fabian asked.

"I will let you decide that among yourselves," the Abbot said. His words were still hanging in the air when the arguing broke out.

There was a time when the other monks would have been concerned about him making such a journey. But they were no longer concerned for each other, only themselves. There was a time when one of the others would have offered to accompany him, but those days were gone.

The Abbot slipped quietly out of the monastery and began his journey toward the mountains. Walking through the forest, in those first miles of his journey, he observed that his heart was anxious. But with each passing mile he became aware of a rising hope in his heart.

As dusk was falling, he came upon a small clearing in the foothills and decided to sleep there for the night. The old monk gathered some wood, made a fire, ate a little bread and cheese, and settled down to sleep.

He was startled in the night by the howling of wolves and the screeching of wild parrots. He noticed his heart was racing, but he was not afraid. He did not fear death, he feared the torture of a life without meaning.

Late the following morning he arrived at the Hermit's cave. The Hermit was standing just outside the cave. As the Abbot approached, he said joyfully, "I have been waiting for you!" and the two men embraced like long-lost brothers.

"I've something to ask you," the Abbot said.

"I know, but that can wait," the Hermit replied. "First, I want to show you something." The Abbot was possessed by an impatience that surprised him, but he followed his old friend.

The two men walked peacefully through the trees

and after about fifteen minutes a fine lake was before them. It was breathtaking.

The Hermit sat on a large boulder at the side of the lake and the Abbot sat on a smaller boulder next to him. They sat in silence for over an hour and the Abbot felt a deep peace rising in his soul.

The lake was clear and still. The surface was like glass and the sun was reflecting perfectly on the water like a golden disc. The Abbot was mesmerized.

When the sun had reached its pinnacle, the Hermit began to speak, "A still pond reflects the sun perfectly. God is the sun. You are the lake. When your soul is still and clear you reflect the truth, beauty, and goodness of God to everyone you encounter. As the day goes on, the wind will pick up, the lake will be full of ripples, and you will barely be able to see the sun's reflection in the water."

After a few minutes the two men walked back through the cypress trees to the cave. As they sat drinking tea the Abbot described what had happened at the monastery over the past several years. The

Hermit listened closely and when the Abbot had finished asked a handful of clarifying questions. "What have you come here to ask?" was the Hermit's last question.

"What wisdom do you have for us? How do we rejuvenate the monastery? How can we best serve the people who come to visit?" the Abbot asked.

"That's three questions," the Hermit said with a smile so radiant that the Abbot had to look away. "I will answer your three questions with one answer," the Hermit continued. "Go back and tell the brothers... the Messiah is among you." And with that the Hermit closed his eyes and slipped into a deep meditation.

"The Messiah is among us, what can that possibly mean?" the Abbot mumbled to himself. But as he walked slowly down the mountains the full meaning of the Hermit's words took root deep in his soul.

Back at the monastery the monks were growing concerned. The Abbot had said he would be gone three days and he had already been gone five days.

The next evening when there was still no sign of him, they began discussing what fate might have befallen him. The following morning Brother Fabian callously suggested he was not coming back either because he had died in the mountains or because he had abandoned them for some other life.

Just as the sun was setting that afternoon Brother Bartholomew saw a figure approaching the monastery and cried out, "We have a visitor." It was not a visitor. It was the Abbot.

He whispered softly to Bartholomew, "Gather everyone in the chapel." The Abbot was radiant as he sat before the whole community on a small wooden stool. He looked 10 years younger. The monks could not remember a time when he seemed so fully alive.

He told the other monks of his journey and shared with them the message he had received, "This is what I asked the Hermit. 'What wisdom do you have for us? How do we rejuvenate the monastery? How can we best serve the people who come to visit?' The Hermit replied, 'That's three questions. I will answer your three questions with one answer. Go back and tell the brothers... the Messiah is among you.'"

The monks were astonished and gasped.

From that moment on they looked at each other differently, they thought of each other differently, and they began to treat each other differently.

The monks wondered day and night who the Messiah among them was. Was it Adrian, Bartholomew, Killian, Owen, Fabian, or was it the Abbot himself? And as the brothers wondered they began to treat each other with renewed kindness and a profound respect.

As time passed the Abbot noticed little things. There was a new spirit of cooperation. The brothers praised and encouraged each other, compassion and forgiveness returned to their hearts, and they were kind to each other.

These little things, these Holy Moments, breathed new life into the community. The monks were flourishing. The monastery was flourishing. Even the flowers in the fields and the cows in the barn seemed happier.

And then one day it happened. The visitors returned. At first it was just one or two visitors like
it had been in the past. But then they brought their
friends, and their friends brought their friends.

Those that came to visit the monastery noticed
that the monks were overflowing with joy. They perceived the monks had a profound reverence for each
other. And they observed the monks' unquenchable
patience with their visitors.

In a few short years the monastery had been transformed from the brink of collapse and was thriving
like never before. A village sprung up around the
monastery, and the monastery became the center of
life for the people of the village. The monks loved the
people, the people loved the monks, and they all lived
together in harmony and happiness.

One Saturday afternoon the old Abbot was sitting
on a bench in the courtyard looking gratefully toward
the mountains, when a woman approached. Sitting
down next to him she asked, "What happened here?"

The old monk beamed his warm, knowing smile

and asked, "What do you mean?"

"This place has been completely transformed," the woman explained.

"No," the Abbot disagreed gently, "the place is exactly the same. It's the monks who have changed."

"How did it happen?" she asked.

"We started living as if the Messiah were among us," the Abbot replied.

The woman pondered that for a moment and then began to weep. The old monk put his arm around her to comfort her. She told him about her life and troubles. The woman shared with him the question that was tormenting her soul, the question that had urged her to visit the monastery. And they sat in silence for a long time.

"What advice do you have for me?" the woman asked, breaking the silence.

The two sat quietly for another long moment before the old man spoke, and then he said, "Treat every person you ever meet like the second coming of Jesus in disguise."

part one

Awakening

MORE TO OFFER

You have so much more to offer. You sense it. You may have known it for a long time. It's a truth that lingers, waiting patiently for us to pay attention to it. It's a soul sense, and when your soul senses such a thing, it should never be ignored.

You may find yourself thinking or saying...

"Something is missing..."

"There must be more to life..."

"I have so much more to offer..."

These are sacred truths. But we often treat them as human malfunctions. We think something is wrong. We think we need to be fixed. We view these sacred truths as problems to be solved, and that is a tragedy.

When you experience these yearnings, something is very, very right! You are not malfunctioning. Nothing could be further from the truth. Your heart, mind, body, and soul are working together to get your attention. These longings are amazing signs that your whole person is functioning beautifully.

When you sense that something is missing, that there must be more to life, or that you have so much more to offer, your intuition has never been so sharp. Claim these as sacred truths about yourself. Listen and follow where they lead.

Each of these yearnings is a summons to live a more meaningful life, an invitation to live life to the fullest, a sacred call to become all you were created to be.

We crave more because we were made for more.

We try to satisfy those cravings with trivial activity and meaningless things. But this foolishness just leaves us exhausted, dissatisfied, and hungrier than ever. These cravings testify in your heart that you were created to strive for more.

Toward the end of his life, Michelangelo observed, "I regret that I have done so little for my eternal soul and that I am but beginning to learn the alphabet of my craft." He was eighty-eight years old and indisputably a genius who had lived a life of astonishing worldly accomplishment. But what was his regret? Care of the soul.

The advantage you have over Michelangelo is that you still have time to do something about it. How much time? Impossible to say, but not enough time to waste any. So, begin today.

You have so much more to offer. But to contribute more, to experience life in new and exciting ways, to accomplish things far beyond your accomplishments so far, and to discover who you really are and what you are here in this world to contribute, you need to start paying closer attention to the sacred truths bubbling up within your soul.

You were made for more. It's time to find out what that "more" is. Holy Moments will draw out your potential.

THE TWO HUNGERS

Are you hungry? What are you hungry for? We're all hungry for something. Knowing what you hunger for is wisdom.

The Bushmen of the Kalahari Desert in Southern Africa talk about "the Two Hungers." There is the Great Hunger and the Little Hunger. The Little Hunger yearns for food while the Great Hunger, the greatest hunger of all, is the hunger for meaning.

"There is ultimately only one thing that makes human beings deeply and profoundly bitter, and that is to have thrust upon them a life without meaning. There is nothing wrong in searching for happiness. But of far more comfort to the soul is something greater than happiness or unhappiness, and that is meaning. Because meaning transfigures all. Once what you are doing has meaning for you, it is irrelevant whether you're happy or unhappy. You are content." This was the beautiful and profound observation of the South African author Laurens van der Post.

We pretend our hunger baffles us. We try to feed

our hunger in a thousand ways, but still our hunger remains, because it will only be satisfied with meaning. We cannot thrive without meaning. Our need for meaning is as urgent and unceasing as our need for water.

Ernest Hemingway was living in Paris when he was trying to make it as a writer. He was young and restless, and wrote about the many yearnings we experience. This was his reflection on a nagging hunger he couldn't satisfy, "My wife and I had a wonderful meal at Michaud's but when we had finished and there was no question of hunger any more the feeling that had been like hunger when we were standing on the bridge was still there. It was there when we came home and after we had gone to bed and made love in the dark, it was there. When I woke with the windows open and the moonlight on the rooftops of Paris, the hunger was still there. I put my face away from the moonlight into the shadow, but I could not sleep and lay awake thinking about it. My wife slept sweetly now with the moonlight on her face. I had to try to think it out. Life had seemed so simple that morning when I had awakened to the spring..."

Have you ever had a night like that? Tossing and turning, wondering about the purpose and direction of your life.

Have you ever had a hunger that would not be satisfied? I suspect we all have.

What are you hungry for in your life right now? Do you know? You may not, and that's okay. We will find out together. But whatever your hunger is, more of the same, more of what you have been trying to satisfy it with until now isn't the answer. Are you open to trying something new?

A MOMENT OF CLARITY

When I was fifteen years old, I had a great spiritual mentor. I don't know how my life would have unfolded if I hadn't met him. But it's difficult to imagine that life would have been anywhere near as fruitful or rewarding as it has been.

He encouraged me to read the Gospels. He taught

me how to pray. He showed me how to care for the poor and visit the lonely. He encouraged me to read great spiritual books. He watched without judgement as I foolishly wrestled with God. He listened patiently to my questions, doubts, excuses, and resistance. And perhaps most of all, he encouraged me to honor those sacred truths that were emerging in my soul: Something is missing, there is more to life, and you do have more to offer.

One of the fruits of this friendship was a moment of clarity so piercing that it has defined my life.

I was walking home from meeting with him one day, when everything we had been discussing for months came together in a single clarifying thought: *Some moments are holy, some moments are unholy, and our choices can guide a moment in either direction.*

It was a rare moment of clarity in a chaotic and confusing world. It was also a moment of intense joy. I can still see myself walking down the street. I know exactly where I was in that moment of awakening.

Everything good in my life has been connected to

that moment. And all the pain and disappointment I have caused myself and others has been the result of abandoning the wisdom that was revealed in that moment.

It only took a moment. In that moment I realized what was possible. In that moment I learned to collaborate with God and create Holy Moments. It was a moment of grace like none other. And I have spent my life trying to help others discover that same clarity and joy. It is the only way I know to express my gratitude for the infinite blessings that moment brought to my life.

It was a moment of awakening, a moment of realization, a moment of discovery, a moment of clarity, and a moment of pure unmitigated joy. It was a Holy Moment.

Now it's your turn. This is your moment. The moment when you realize that despite what your life has been up until now, and regardless of anything you have done in the past, what matters most is what you do next.

WHEN LIFE FINALLY MAKES SENSE

Once we discover that some moments are holy, some moments are unholy, and our choices can guide a moment in either direction, life finally begins to make sense.

This is no small thing. Most people in the modern secular world cannot make sense of life. The culture has exiled them from God, religion, and spirituality. So, each day is a frustrated attempt to put together the jigsaw puzzle of life without crucial pieces. We are baffled by life. This bewilderment is deeply personal, because we are not only struggling to make sense of life in general, but we are struggling to make sense of our own lives.

The more disconnected from God our lives become the more meaningless life becomes.

Holy Moments give meaning and divine purpose to our lives. Meaning is crucial to our health and happiness. We cannot thrive as human beings without it. And we cannot live a meaningful life by filling our life with trivial things and meaningless activities. Holy Moments solve the meaninglessness of our lives.

There is a moment at the end of each day, when we lay our heads on our pillows. Our bodies are tired, our minds relax, and our egos let go. It is a solitary moment. If we listen carefully in that moment, we will discover where we stand. Where we stand with God, where we stand with those we love, and where we stand with our truest self. That moment never lies. It reveals the meaning or meaninglessness of our lives.

Meaning binds your life together into one coherent whole. It connects all the many aspects of your life. We live more vigorously and courageously when we are able to connect our daily activity with the greater meaning and purpose of life.

The simple truth that some moments are holy, some moments are unholy, and our choices can guide a moment in either direction, reveals the profound meaning that each and every human act contains. This one idea holds the power to bring meaning and purpose to every moment of your life.

Holy Moments inject meaning into every moment of your life.

WHAT IS A HOLY MOMENT?

We have established that some moments are holy, some moments are unholy, and our choices can guide a moment in either direction.

We have established that our ability to guide moments toward what is holy demonstrates that each and every human act contains profound meaning.

Now, let us explore exactly how "our choices can guide a moment," for this is the essence of collaborating with God to create Holy Moments.

The crucial question is: What is a Holy Moment?

A Holy Moment is a single moment in which you open yourself to God. You make yourself available to Him. You set aside personal preference and self-interest, and for one moment you do what you prayerfully believe God is calling you to do.

These Holy Moments, these tiny collaborations with God, unleash the pure unmitigated joy that I first experienced walking home that afternoon when I was fifteen. The same pure unmitigated joy that is about to flood every corner of your being.

So, begin today. One of the beautiful things about this idea is that you can implement it immediately. You do not need to study it for years. No special qualifications are necessary. This alone demonstrates the power of the Holy Moments principle.

You are equipped right now to collaborate with God and create Holy Moments. The coming pages will teach you how to recognize opportunities to create Holy Moments in any situation; show you how to practically apply the principle in your daily life; connect you with the meaning and purpose of your one short life; and flood your relationships with goodness. But you know everything you need to know right now to begin activating Holy Moments in your life.

You can begin today.

And here's the beautiful thing. If you can collaborate with God today to create one Holy Moment, you can create two tomorrow, and four the next day, and eight the day after that. There is no limit to the number of Holy Moments you can participate in.

THE MOMENT OF DECISION

If you only learn to master one moment in your life, learn to master the moment of decision.

We all make choices. That's the easy part. The hard thing about choices is living with them. We all have regrets. We have all said and done things that we would do differently if we could go back in time. We know we can't. We may have made peace with those choices to some extent, but still, in the quiet hours they haunt us.

If I could give only one piece of advice, it would be this: Make choices that are easy to live with. Make choices you can look back on longingly, like you do upon the best of times with the best of friends.

Life is choices. We are constantly making them. But are we choosing wisely? We are not born great decision makers. It is something that must be learned.

The wisdom of Holy Moments will teach you how to become a great decision maker.

When you have a decision to make, consult your future self. Imagine yourself twenty years from now, looking back on this moment, and honor what your future self advises you to do.

A young man decided one Thursday night to rob a convenience store with his friends. Only something went horribly wrong. The cashier ended up dead and the young man was sentenced to life in prison. He never intended to use the gun when he bought it. He set the gun on the counter during the robbery, and it went off. For more than forty years he played that moment over and again in his mind. He wanted to know what happened, what went wrong. But memories fade and all we are left with are the consequences of the choices we have made.

"Every day I feel regret. I was nineteen then and I am sixty-two now. Forty-three years, locked up in a cage. Some days I can taste the regret in my mouth when I wake up. Other days, I will almost make it through the whole day, and then the smallest reminder will trigger a memory, and the memory will trigger the regret. That kind of regret, even after all these years, is like being punched in the stomach by a gorilla. I ask myself over and over: Why? I didn't need the money. I mean I didn't have any money, but I didn't really need the money. We were just kids being stupid in a grown-up world. I wish I could go back and change just one moment of my life. Change that one decision and my whole life would have been different. I wish I could go back and talk to the young man I was the day I bought that gun. I wish I could tell that young man, 'Stay home tonight.' But I can't."

That's what regret sounds like. I have my own regrets. We all do.

Regrets teach us that choices have consequences. Regrets reveal that we need to become better decision makers.

We teach little children that choices have consequences. It is one of life's fundamental truths. But adults often adopt the temporary insanity of imagining that our choices will only have the consequences we intend. But it is the unintended consequences of our choices that often wreak havoc in our lives and the lives of other people.

Choices have consequences. We know that. But we throw this indisputable truth aside in order to deny the consequences of our unholy moments. But by denying that our choices have consequences, we abandon our power to create Holy Moments, and render ourselves spiritually impotent.

When we teach children that choices have consequences, the emphasis is usually placed on the consequences of poor choices, while the powerful and positive consequences of wise choices are often overlooked.

Holy Moments are choices with powerful and positive consequences. Holy Moments are choices that are easy to live with.

It's time to start filling our lives with Holy Moments. If you glance back at your life, the choices you find hardest to live with were unholy moments. And the choices you find easiest to live with, the ones you are rightly proud of, those you cherish, they each held the seed of goodness. They were Holy Moments.

Decision making is a powerful force in our lives. Our decisions quite literally shape our lives. We make the future with our choices.

The beautiful thing about choices is you have more to make. Choices got you here, but if you don't like "here" all you need to do is start making different choices.

Your choices have power.

If someone had an incredible power and used it for evil that would be a horrible thing. But what about if someone had an incredible power and didn't use it for good? There's something tragic and wrong about that too, isn't there?

That someone is you. You possess an incredible power. You can choose what is good and holy or you can choose what is unholy and destructive. Your choices have power.

THE REST OF YOUR LIFE

So, let me ask you: What are you going to do with the rest of your life?

More of the same? Continue to distract yourself with meaningless nonsense? Focus on what you can get? Keep dreaming about a change you know you will never make? Or are you finally, once and for all, ready to do something about the nagging dissatisfaction in your soul?

You have one short life. We all waste some of it. How much are you wasting?

If you are ready for a change, it only takes a handful of Holy Moments to flood your soul with joy and show you a new and exciting vision of the rest of your life.

There is a beautiful story in Matthew's Gospel where Jesus takes Peter, James, and John up a high mountain. There he was transfigured. His face shone like the sun, and His clothes became as white as light.

The definition of transfiguration is a complete change of appearance into a more beautiful spiritual state. Each Holy Moment is a mini-transfiguration. Holy Moments allow us to see what is possible, even if only for a fleeting moment. Each Holy Moment reveals who you are capable of being, and who you are capable of being is amazing.

So, don't let your past rob you of your future. You are more than the worst thing that has ever happened to you. You are more than the worst thing you have ever done. God is never more than one choice away. It only takes one Holy Moment to shift the momentum of your life in the right direction.

The rest of your life is waiting for you. It will be filled with moments. Will they be Holy Moments or unholy moments? The choice is yours.

part two

Holy Moments Explained

AN ICON OF GOODNESS

A man was traveling from Jerusalem to Jericho, when he was seized by robbers, who stripped him, beat him, and went away, leaving him half dead. Now by chance a priest was going down that road; and when he saw him, he passed by on the other side. In the same way, a scholar was traveling by the path, when he came to the place and saw the man laying beaten by the side of the road, he looked away and quickly passed by on the other side. But a Samaritan traveling in the region saw the man and approached him. Seeing that he was naked and badly beaten, the Samaritan was moved with pity. He took the wounded man in his arms, treated his wounds with wine and soothed them with oil, and then bandaged them. The Samaritan put the unfortunate man on his donkey, brought him to an inn, and took care of him. The next day he took money from his own purse, gave it to the innkeeper, and said, "Take care of him. When I return, I will repay you whatever more you spend."

The Good Samaritan is legendary. He is a worldwide icon of goodness. He is recognized by believers and non-believers alike.

Anytime someone goes out of his or her way to selflessly help others, especially a stranger who is in need, we refer to that person as a Good Samaritan. Even secular media outlets use the term.

The Good Samaritan is the patron saint of Holy Moments.

What the Good Samaritan did was a spectacular Holy Moment. But it's important to understand that his character was predisposed to that action. His soul had been prepared with hundreds of choices and decisions before that day. His heart was gently inclined toward the needs of others. The other men who didn't stop to help the stranger in distress had their reasons for not stopping. I wonder what their hearts were inclined toward.

Is your heart inclined toward the needs of others? Or is it leaning away from others?

The world needs more Good Samaritans. The world needs more Holy Moments. The world needs you and me to collaborate with God (and each other) to create those Holy Moments.

HOW TO FILL YOUR LIFE WITH HOLY MOMENTS

You are probably yearning to know a little more about Holy Moments, and specifically, how you can begin to activate them in your life. That's the Holy Spirit stirring within you. Our hunger for goodness comes from God.

Let's break down a Holy Moment, line by line, concept by concept.

A Holy Moment is a single moment in which you open yourself to God. You make yourself available to Him. You set aside personal preference and self-interest, and for one moment you do what you prayerfully believe God is calling you to do.

"A Holy Moment is a single moment."

The beauty of a single moment is that it's not overwhelming. It's not a day, a week, a month, or even a whole hour. It's just one moment. In that one moment you discover what you are capable of doing and who you are capable of being. Both discoveries will amaze you.

"...in which you open yourself to God."

Are you open to God? Sometimes we are and sometimes we aren't. We can be open to God in some areas of our lives, but closed to Him in other areas of our lives. Holy Moments give us the chance to experience what it's like to be 100% open to God, because no matter who we are or what we have done in the past, we are all capable of opening ourselves 100% to God for a single moment.

"You make yourself available to Him."

If you want to see miracles, make yourself available

to God. When we make ourselves available to God amazing things happen. Throughout history God has collaborated with the most unlikely people to make amazing things happen, and now He wants to collaborate with you. God almost never chooses the most qualified person or the people in positions of power and authority. God chooses people nobody would expect.

When God is looking for someone to collaborate with, He chooses those who make themselves available to Him. He does not see your past as an impediment to your future. The rest of your life begins the moment you make yourself available to God.

"You set aside personal preference..."

Personal preferences are great. We prefer certain types of food, music, chocolate, movies, sports, books, animals, and cities. We all have personal preferences. Tons of them. But our preferences don't stop here. We prefer specific outcomes in situations. We have preferences about what people say and do. And all these preferences can become self-serving and blind us to what is best.

God may desire what you desire. God's preference may be the same as your preference. But in order to find out, we need to set aside our personal preferences, so we can look at a situation through God's eyes.

"You set aside... self-interest."

Why do we cling so tightly to self-interest? We aggressively defend and pursue self-interest because we believe if we don't look out for ourselves nobody else will. It is the fruit of the "every man for himself" ethos. It has its roots in Medieval times, having first appeared in Chaucer's *The Knight's Tale* in the late 1300s, but remains deeply embedded in today's culture.

This approach is a fundamental denial of God's providence. "God will not take care of me, so I have to take care of myself," is what it really proclaims.

God is more committed to your happiness and flourishing than anybody. But getting what you want doesn't make you happy. You know that and God never forgets it. What is good for you is better than what you want.

The more we evolve spiritually, the more we want what is good for us. Learning to desire what is good for you requires getting beyond your personal preferences and self-interest. This is essential to bring about alignment between God's desires and your desires. And every Holy Moment you create with God strengthens this alignment.

You can set your self-interest aside. God always has your best interest in mind. But, keep in mind, we are only talking about a single moment here. And yet, each time you set aside your self-interest for a Holy Moment, you will discover that it is safe and your trust in God will grow.

"...and for one moment..."
The idea that leads most addicts to relapse is the idea that they can never do "it" again. Alcoholics in recovery are taught not to think about never having a drink ever again. They are encouraged to take life one day at a time. Those that are successful with this approach find themselves stringing together months and years and decades of newfound happiness and sobriety.

We're just talking about a single moment here. One Holy Moment. We're not even taking life one day at a time. We are taking life one moment at a time. It's essential to remember this at every point in our journey together.

We are simply trying to find out what is possible in a single moment. Once we understand the power and possibilities that a single moment holds, it soon dawns on us what stringing a few of these moments together could accomplish.

"...you do..."

Holy Moments are active, not passive. They don't just happen. We make them happen in collaboration with God. We choose them. A Holy Moment is a grace-filled, prayer-directed action.

"...what you prayerfully believe..."

Prayer-guided action is powerful. Seek God's counsel before you act. The Holy Spirit yearns to coach, mentor, advise, and guide you every moment of your life. I have never met anyone who relied too much on the Holy Spirit, though I often rely too little on Him.

"God is calling you to do."

God is calling you every day to new adventures and opportunities. He often sends them disguised as opportunities for Holy Moments. The Holy Spirit wants to guide you in wisdom in each moment of the day. When we listen to the voice of God, and do what God is calling us to do, we live deeply fulfilling lives and our souls erupt with joy.

There are so many things that we cannot change in this troubled world. When we focus on the negative our energy is quickly drained. We become anxious, stressed, overwhelmed, and exhausted, because it is demoralizing to feel helpless. But we are not helpless.

The power of Holy Moments demonstrates that we are the opposite of helpless. The principle of Holy Moments teaches us to focus on the good we can do. This energizes us. Some moments are holy, some moments are unholy, and our choices can guide a moment in either direction. This is an enormously empowering truth.

Let Holy Moments show you what is possible.

EVERYDAY EXAMPLES OF
HOLY MOMENTS

How many situations do you see each day in need of a Holy Moment?

One of the things I love about this idea is how universally practical it is. It can be applied to every situation in every aspect of our lives. In a workshop recently, I asked the group to put together a list of the ten aspects of life that mattered most. This is what they came up with: Health, Marriage and Family, Work, Spirituality, Home Life, Finances, Friendships, Recreation, Community, and Personal Growth.

Holy Moments can be applied to each of these aspects of our lives, and Holy Moments will improve all of these aspects of our lives.

Holy Moments make us better husbands and wives, parents and children, friends and neighbors, brothers and sisters, colleagues and citizens. Holy Moments make us better human beings.

That's why everywhere you go you will see opportunities for Holy Moments. This isn't just a theory; it can be activated to improve every aspect of our lives.

My son Walter came into my office this evening to say goodnight as I was working on this manuscript. He asked what I was working on and I explained. "Did you have any Holy Moments today?" I asked him. He thought for a minute and then replied, "I'm not sure." Earlier that day I was driving him home and he said, "Do you think we should stop and get Ralph some donuts?" Walter doesn't care for donuts, but his little brother Ralph loves donuts. So, we stopped and got him some. Now I said to Walter, "That was a Holy Moment driving home today when you suggested we get some donuts for your brother. That was very thoughtful, and I am so proud of you." Walter glowed. We got home to discover that little Ralphie was having a tough day. But when his big brother walked through the door and gave him the donuts he beamed, and I could see his spirits beginning to rise. It was a little thing. A tiny thing. And that's what we forget, little things can make a big difference.

Let's look at more real-life examples of Holy Moments.

John Miller discovered that his neighbor three houses down had broken his leg. He had never met this neighbor, but on Saturday when he was mowing his lawn, he noticed the lawn three houses down was getting a little long. So, when he was finished mowing his own, he went down and mowed his neighbor's lawn. That was a Holy Moment.

Mary Wright goes through the drive-through to get coffee each Friday morning and pays for the person behind her. When I asked her why, she replied, "So many reasons, I guess. We need to look out for each other. Lots of people have been generous to me. People need to know that there are generous, thoughtful people in the world. And ultimately, I believe that thoughtfulness and generosity are contagious and can change the world." That's one of Mary's Holy Moments. And she's right—Holy Moments are contagious.

Lillian Lopez thought she was going to lose her mind over her teenage daughter's attitude and behavior. She had prayed for months asking God to do something, but it turned out God wanted Lillian to do something. The following Sunday morning, she woke her daughter at 7:00 a.m., saying, "Get yourself ready; we are leaving in twenty minutes." As you can imagine, that wasn't too well received. "Where are we going?" her daughter yelled. "I'll tell you on the way," her mother replied. Earlier in the week Lillian had bought two leather-bound journals. They weren't expensive, but money was tight, so they didn't come without sacrifice. Lillian took her daughter to their favorite breakfast spot. After they had ordered, she pushed one of the journals across the table. "What's this?" her daughter asked. "It's the book of your life," Lillian answered. "A place to write your hopes and dreams, a place to plan, and somewhere to doodle when doodling is what best helps you think about your future." Her daughter's eyes began to fill with tears. It was a Holy Moment. "So, what are your dreams?" Lillian asked her daughter. They talked for almost two hours about her daughter's hopes and dreams for her life, and she started writing them in her journal. Then Lillian's daughter noticed the second journal. "What's the other journal?" she asked her mother. That was another Holy Moment. "That's my book of life," Lillian replied. "It's time for me to start dreaming again too."

Joan Binzer worked at a greeting card company. Less than three miles from the company was a prison with four hundred male occupants, the worst of the worst offenders. Joan had worked at the greeting card company for thirteen years, and every morning as she drove past the prison, she wondered about the prisoners and what had gone wrong in their lives. As a mother, she couldn't help but think how hard it must be for their mothers. As May came around that year, Joan had an idea. She went to her boss and said, "What if for our community service project this quarter, we take some Mother's Day cards and stamps over to the prison for the prisoners to send to their moms?" Joan's boss said he would check with the prison and get back to her. The following week he told Joan the prison warden was very appreciative and supportive. So, Joan and nine of her colleagues went over to the prison with two hundred Mother's Day cards, thinking that not all the prisoners would necessarily want to participate. It quickly became apparent that her assumption was completely wrong. Before Joan had helped a dozen prisoners pick a card for their mothers, she had been asked seven times, "Would it be OK if I took two?" Joan finally worked up the nerve to ask one of the prisoners, "What is your name, sir?" "Jimmy Johnson, ma'am!" he replied. "Why do you want two, Jimmy?" Joan asked. "Well, my mom did the best she could, but she had her own problems, and so I was mostly raised by my grandmother. So, I was thinking if it was okay with you good people, I would send one to my grandmother too!" Joan had to use all her strength not to burst into tears. There were four hundred inmates in the prison that day, and every single one wrote a Mother's Day card. That's four hundred Holy Moments. In fact, Joan and her company ended up mailing 657 Mother's Day cards for the inmates.

⁙ ◉ ⁙

Tony Harris discovered something about himself: He is a very impatient listener. He constantly finds himself wanting to jump in, interrupt, and make a point. For the past four years, he has been consciously trying to become a more patient listener. That's a lot of patient Holy Moments. "Just by focusing on changing this one horrible habit I developed over my life, I find I am more patient with my wife, my children, my colleagues at work, my pastor, the strangers who cross my path, even the people who really irritate me." Holy Moments cannot be contained. They reach out into every relationship and aspect of our lives.

Anastasia Petrov is a Russian immigrant and a nurse. "I love America," she says to me with her sixty-two-year-old smile. A few years ago, one of the other nurses at the hospital got cancer and had to take some time off work. Anastasia didn't know her very well, but she knew that the other nurse had three kids and that she needed to work. The hospital's policy allowed for the sick nurse to have six weeks off with pay, but after that her time away from work was without pay. At lunch one day Anastasia heard some of the other nurses talking about doing one of those online funding projects to help out. "We can do better than that!" Anastasia said to her colleagues. They all turned and stared at her in surprise. You see, Anastasia was a quiet woman. She was a listener. Plenty of lunch breaks would pass without her saying a single word. Perhaps it was just her personality, or maybe it was the result of being raised in Russia under the weight of Communism. "What do you mean?" one of her colleagues finally asked. "Everyone loves Jane [the sick nurse]. She is always doing kind things for people. Each nurse has three twelve-hour shifts a week. All we need to do is find three nurses each week to volunteer to do an extra shift." The other nurses stared at her with astonishment and admiration. "I'll organize the schedule," Anastasia added. And so she did. Each week while Jane was off work, Anastasia found three nurses to do an extra shift so that Jane could continue to be paid her full salary. I learned about this from Sophia, another nurse at the hospital. "How long was Jane off from work?" I asked Sophia. "Three years!" she replied with a smile. "Anastasia is a saint," she continued. Talk about Holy Moments. I figure Anastasia triggered about ten million Holy Moments at lunch that day.

Holy Moments come in all shapes and sizes. Here are some more everyday examples:

Control your temper, even if you are fully justified in losing it.

Pray before making a decision.

Encourage someone, coach someone, praise someone, affirm someone.

Be patient with that person who drives you crazy.

Do something that helps you become a-better-version-of-yourself, even when you don't feel like it.

Give whoever is in front of you your full attention. That's a Holy Moment.

Begin each day with a short prayer of gratitude.

Catch someone doing something right and praise them.

Overlook an offense against you.

Go out of your way to make the new person feel welcome.

Take your spouse's car and fill it with gas.

Take an interest in someone: Ask him about the best part of his day; ask her about her dreams.

Give someone a life-changing book.

Stand up for someone who is being bullied or be-littled.

Write a love letter.

Clean up the mess even though you didn't make it.

Express your appreciation to someone who helps you.

Pray for the people who are having the hardest day of their lives right now.

Teach someone about Holy Moments. An easy way to do that is to give someone a copy of this book. Teaching someone about Holy Moments could trigger thousands of Holy Moments. We will send you the book. Just visit HolyMomentsBook.com and request six free copies of this book to share with others. Imagine how many Holy Moments you will trigger in a person's life by introducing them to this idea.

These are all examples of every day Holy Moments. There are some amazing stories here, but Holy Moments come in all shapes and sizes, and most of them are small and anonymous. The important takeaway is the realization that Holy Moments are possible. Not just for other people, but for you. That is an amazing discovery.

Every day you will see opportunities for Holy Moments. These opportunities are literally everywhere. There is a way to respond to every situation that transforms it into a Holy Moment. And there is nothing more fulfilling than collaborating with God to create Holy Moments.

Holy Moments are going to make you insanely happy.

WHY DO HOLY MOMENTS MAKE US SO HAPPY?

Feeling good is an amazing thing. It shouldn't be our goal in life but feeling good has its purpose. God invented feeling good for a reason.

Things that feel good often draw us toward the fullest expression of our potential as human beings. Those good feelings are breadcrumbs designed to lead us toward what is morally good and good for us.

When we are doing what is good for us and what is morally good we experience an undeniable sense of fulfillment. The ultimate feel-good sensations come from aligning our lives with what is good, true, right, just, and noble.

Holy Moments feel good. They make us incredibly happy. You are not imagining it, and it's not just metaphorical. Every Holy Moment is an act of generosity, and scientists have discovered that generosity releases three hormones that are critical for a human being to flourish.

The first is serotonin. This regulates happiness and mood in general.

The second is dopamine. This is responsible for allowing us to experience pleasure, satisfaction, and motivation.

And the third is oxytocin. This is the hormone that is released during childbirth, sex, breastfeeding, exercise, while hugging, holding hands, listening to music, and sharing a meal with friends.

Holy Moments release oxytocin into the

bloodstream, inducing feelings of warmth, euphoria, and connection with others. Holy Moments literally produce a natural oxytocin high, and that is one of the reasons it feels so good to collaborate with God to create Holy Moments.

These three God-made hormones are so powerful that they allow us to experience joy even while suffering. This explains why even from prison, the apostle Paul wrote more about joy than any other theme. Let's face it, some Holy Moments come at great personal sacrifice. The satisfaction derived from Holy Moments can even supersede physical suffering. Women experience a similar phenomenon during childbirth.

Holy Moments also have a myriad of other positive effects on us. They boost feelings of confidence, optimism, and the general sense that our lives are moving in a positive direction. Holy Moments also liberate us from feeling helpless. Holy Moments move us from a passive state (waiting for something good to happen), to an active state (making something good happen).

We have been marvelously created. The way our

whole being responds to creating Holy Moments encourages us to create more; and with every Holy Moment you become more perfectly yourself, your relationships become healthier, and you contribute to a more positive society.

Holy Moments bring about flourishing for everyone, everywhere, in every sense of the word. So, it is only natural that they would make us happy.

YOUR TIDAL WAVE OF GOODNESS

Holy Moments are one of the most powerful forces on earth. One seemingly insignificant Holy Moment can produce a tidal wave of goodness.

There are no small acts. No act infused with goodness can ever be considered small. Every act of goodness triggers more goodness. Each act, however small, sets in place a chain reaction of Holy Moments. You never know who will be impacted by the succession of Holy Moments you begin. Your Holy Moments will produce tremendous ripple effects.

I know it. I believe it. I have seen it. I am it.

I began this book by briefly mentioning one of my spiritual mentors. He encouraged me to delve deeper into life's possibilities. Those Holy Moments were the catalyst that began on the other side of the world in Australia.

That man triggered a tidal wave of goodness. He inspired me, and in turn, all the people who have read my books, attended my presentations, watched my YouTube videos, have been inspired by the ripple effect. His tidal wave of goodness is easily seen in my public life as an author and speaker. But his tidal wave of goodness has also deeply impacted my personal life. My friendships, marriage, parenting, community involvement, relationships with colleagues, and the simple Holy Moments I participate in each day have all been touched by his goodness. He invested in me and the evidence of the goodness he set in motion is everywhere in my life.

My life has unleashed a tidal wave of goodness around the world. That may sound prideful and arrogant. It isn't. I know who made it happen. I'm not confused about who the credit belongs to. It was a collaboration with God and so many other people. I can take pleasure in the fact that I got to be part of it, but to take prideful credit would be foolish.

My parents and teachers, brothers and friends, coaches and pastors, all helped set this tidal wave of goodness in motion. I was the beneficiary of their Holy Moments.

Sometimes when I have a few moments to spare in an airport, I look at the screens that list all the cities. I can see the faces of the people in each city who helped make this happen. I cannot describe the feeling. My heart is bursting with awe and gratitude in those moments, and as I turn and make my way to my flight, I whisper a prayer for all those people and their families.

I know the goodness of God is the essential catalyst in every Holy Moment. And yet, it is important to acknowledge that I played a role in it all, because acknowledging that shows others what is possible.

But let me tell you the best news of all. I am weak

and broken, fragile and wounded. I have made horrible mistakes in my life. I have taken wrong turns and compounded those wrong turns with arrogance and stubbornness. I have been selfish. I have put my wants ahead of other people's needs. There have been plenty of unholy moments in my life. But the unholy moments of our past don't prevent us from creating Holy Moments in the future.

Why is all this good news? It proves that you can unleash a tidal wave of goodness with your life too.

How do you begin? It starts in the same way for every person, with one Holy Moment. How does it continue? One Holy Moment at a time.

part three

The Divine Plan

WHAT GIVES YOU HOPE?

To write is to hope. My main hope in setting out to write this book was to convince you of one thing: Holy Moments are possible. I knew if I could convince you of that your life would change. Sometimes a reader will say, "Your book changed my life!" It is beautiful and humbling to hear, but the danger is to think of the book as the miracle. The real miracle is the changed life.

Holy Moments are possible. If that statement is true, so many other things become possible.

There is an amazing moment in Victor Hugo's epic story *Les Misérables*. The main character is a man named Jean Valjean. Released from prison after nineteen years of hard labor for stealing a loaf of bread, he is bitter, angry, and resentful of everyone. One evening he knocks on a door looking for food. The owner welcomes him into his home to share a meal and to stay the night.

Valjean repays this generous hospitality by stealing his host's silverware. The police capture him the next day and bring him back to return the silverware. But Valjean's host protects his thieving guest, telling the police that the silverware was a gift. This act of kindness, this Holy Moment, sets Valjean free in every way imaginable.

Jean Valjean's host was an elderly bishop, a true man of God. He knew Holy Moments had the power to ransom people from fear and hatred and return them to God.

This encounter with the bishop was the first time in decades Valjean had been treated with love, respect, and compassion. It forever changes him.

It was a moment of tender care. The bishop did not see Valjean as a thief and he did not see himself as a bishop. He saw only two brothers. In that moment nothing else mattered to him except what was best for Jean Valjean. It was indeed a Holy Moment.

This one moment of brotherly love set off a domino effect of goodness. As a result of the bishop's goodness, the effect of that one Holy Moment, Valjean unleashes an astonishing wave of Holy Moments everywhere he goes for the rest of his life. These Holy Moments touch thousands of lives and transform a whole town.

Valjean was hopeless. Devastated by hatred and injustice, having suffered so much throughout his life, he had lost faith in himself, in others, in God, and in society. One man restored his hope in one moment, and Jean Valjean was able to change and go on to become a universal symbol of redemption and hope.

Like in *Les Misérables*, there is so much hopelessness in the world today. Like Jean Valjean, many people today have lost hope. Discouraged and confused, too many people are miserable.

What gives you hope? This is one of the most

common questions people asked as I traveled around the world. I didn't realize it at first, but as the question kept coming up, I started paying attention to who was asking. I discovered it was usually good people who were losing hope.

I have now asked hundreds of people the question myself: What gives you hope? Over the years, since I started asking this question, I have noticed people are taking longer to answer. And sadly, more people don't have an answer at all. Hope has evaporated from so many people's lives.

What is hope? It is the belief that good things lay ahead. It is a combination of desire and expectation. It is the confidence that something wonderful is possible.

When we enter into hopelessness, even our ability to desire good things diminishes, and all our expectations turn negative.

There are a growing number of people who have lost hope in our society. Devastated by cruelty and injustice, having suffered in so many ways, they have lost faith in themselves, in humanity, in God, and in society. Just like Jean Valjean they need the tender touch of a Holy Moment.

What's the difference between when we are hopeful and hopeless? When we are hopeful, we believe the future can be better than the past and that there are things we can do to help bring about that better future. Hope empowers us.

When we lose hope, we stop believing the future can be better, and start believing that there is nothing we can do about our situation. This victim mindset takes us deeper into the hopelessness, which makes us feel that even the smallest things are impossible.

Holy Moments remind us that the future can be better than the past. They fill us with hope. They show us that we have a vital role to play in bringing about that better future. Holy Moments empower us to give others the gift of hope, and the ability to give other people hope is profoundly beautiful.

Anything that can bring people hope is of infinite value. Holy Moments are such a thing.

THE WORLD IS A MESS

The world is a mess. I could quote statistics, but it isn't necessary. Your own experience confirms this sad truth.

I am concerned about the world my children are growing up in. It makes me anxious to think about the world that will greet our grandchildren if we continue down the path our society is on.

What happened? How did it get this way? The short answer: Unholy moments. The uncomfortable answer: Our unholy moments. Yours, mine, everyone's, all the way back to Adam and Eve. This simple truth forces us to acknowledge our personal responsibility.

The sad thing is every unholy moment makes us less of who we were created to be, and every unholy moment makes the world a little more of a mess. When we abandon our destiny, we harm ourselves and others, make happiness impossible, and leave behind us a trail of collateral damage.

We cause most of the world's problems. It's a blunt

truth, but a truth nonetheless. We are the creators of much of our own misery and the cause of much of other people's unhappiness.

The world is a bit of a mess, there's no denying it, but we can do something about it. And if there is one thing that Holy Moments announces boldly it is this, "You can do something about it." That's right, *you* can do something about it. Don't underestimate yourself, God doesn't!

Holy Moments are the solution to the world's problems. This great collaboration between God and humanity is the untested solution to our problems. Unholy moments got us into this mess and only Holy Moments will get us out of it.

THE PROGRESS DELUSION

"The world has been a mess for a long time," is some people's excuse. "The world will always be a mess," is other people's excuse. The world may always be a mess, but that doesn't mean we shouldn't strive to make it a little less messy.

One thing is clear: What we are doing isn't working and we need a new approach.

For too long we have been under the spell of the progress delusion. The progress delusion is the misguided belief that change and progress are the same thing. All change is not progress.

What is progress? Improving the well-being of human beings. What is the purpose of progress? Human flourishing. But not everyone who proposes progress has human flourishing as their goal. Some are more interested in personal achievement, political power, and economic gain than they are in bringing about the most good for the most people.

A great deal of good has been accomplished in the name of progress. Examples include greater life expectancy, reduced infant mortality, expanding food supply, safe water for much of the world, and access to education and healthcare. But the abuse of workers, the exploitation of poorer nations, the devastating atrocities of war, genocide, and environmental extortion have also been perpetrated under the banner of "progress."

We have also been too quick to declare victory in our quest for progress. Consider the phones we carry in our pockets. We have more communication than ever before and this is hailed as progress, but do we have better relationships? Better relationships would be human flourishing. But even the most casual observer comes to the conclusion that these devices have wreaked havoc on our lives and relationships.

If the goal of progress is to improve the well-being of people and bring about human flourishing, how can something that dehumanizes people be considered progress?

Social media is another example. It has been directly linked to anxiety and depression caused by isolation. This is the exact opposite of what it claims to do. It claims to improve our relationships when in fact it destroys them and dehumanizes people in the process.

Just like a gambling addict, we exaggerate our wins and ignore our losses in our so-called quest for progress.

We hail our latest technological advancement as an unqualified success, but there are uncomfortable truths that confront our claims of progress. One billion people on our planet are chronically hungry. This is the sanitized term we use to avoid saying they are starving to death. Two billion people don't have safe drinking water in their homes. Twenty people are the victims of domestic violence every minute. One in three of our daughters and sons are sexually assaulted by the age of thirty. Someone is murdered every minute. And all this before we consider the ravages of war and environmental degradation.

These facts suggest that our untested assumptions of ongoing progress are either overstated or based on the wrong outcomes. These disturbing facts also remind us that when it comes to the human family and life on this planet, there is one essential principle: Our destinies are linked.

But the greatest failure of this so-called progress is spiritual. Genuine progress leads to the flourishing of the entire human person, it does not reduce people to economic tools or social animals. The deformed breed of progress being championed in our society today has caused the spiritual annihilation of generations of men, women, and children. This spiritual genocide is a crime against humanity, and therefore, anything but progress.

Perhaps it's time to reconsider our entire approach to progress.

All progress involves change, but not all change is progress. Change is inevitable, progress is not. History demonstrates this repeatedly with the demise and extinction of whole civilizations. Change can just as easily lead to stagnation, regression, deterioration, and extinction. These alternatives make it clear that discerning the path that leads to genuine progress is one of the great challenges every society faces (and every person).

Our ability to meet this challenge rests upon our moral and spiritual qualities. Many people would like to believe that progress is solely dependent on our intellectual capacity to innovate and that our moral character is irrelevant to the quest. This simply isn't true. To look beyond our own selfish interests and toward the common good, with a goal of accomplishing the most good for the most people, moral character is not only necessary it is essential. The idea of genuine progress being accomplished by people who are morally indifferent is lunacy.

The culture's aggression toward morality and dismissal of anything spiritual will be the major obstacles to progress in society from this moment onward. A people confused about the difference between right and wrong, good and bad, just and unjust, will grasp at anything that promises progress and find themselves bouncing from one oblivion to another.

Determining what will cause society to flourish begins with acknowledging what causes an individual human being to flourish.

Our lives only genuinely improve when we grow in virtue. The virtue of patience improves our lives. It improves our relationships. Two patient people will always have a better relationship than two impatient

people. The same is true for generosity, perseverance, compassion, humility and courage. Growing in virtue leads to the personal and spiritual expansion that are the hallmarks of human flourishing.

You cannot improve your life in any meaningful way without improving as a human being. And what is true for one person is true for an entire society. Virtue is the only way for a society to make genuine progress.

Virtues are the building blocks of character. "Character is destiny," the Greek philosopher Heraclitus observed. This is true for a person, a marriage, a family, community, nation, and indeed, the whole human collective. Character is moral and ethical excellence, it is built one virtue upon another, and the progress of the human race depends upon it.

We look to science, technology, education, and economic growth as the champions of progress. These each have a role to play, but their success in bringing about human flourishing rests upon the virtue and character of the people driving these initiatives.

People keep insisting on progress, but maybe we should consider a new approach. What will bring about the human flourishing that progress promises but so rarely delivers? Holy Moments. Which of our problems would not be solved if we could summon enough Holy Moments?

The next great wave of progress will be the fruit of our compassion, generosity, love, patience, kindness, discipline, gentleness, forgiveness, empathy, and friendship. Not technology. Not economics. Not innovation. Not politics. The progress we desperately need will only be achieved with Holy Moments.

WE NEED A NEW APPROACH

We need a new approach if we are going to solve the world's problems and ease the pain so many people experience daily. And while this new approach may be new to us, it is ancient. Holy Moments are as old as time itself.

Our bias toward new and different is so strong that we overlook tried and true. Our unbridled love

affair with the idea of progress leads us away from ancient solutions to timeless problems.

What we need is the spiritual awareness to recognize opportunities for Holy Moments and the spiritual intelligence to bring them about. This is what leads to meaningful lives, enriched relationships, and a better world for everyone.

Experts agree that Emotional Intelligence (EQ) is disappearing from our culture at an alarming rate. It has become clear that EQ is a better predictor of success than IQ, both personally and professionally. These are important discoveries. But when will we begin the epic conversation that our culture so desperately needs around Spiritual Intelligence (SQ)?

Spirituality provides the tools necessary to develop empathy, temperament, impulse control, sustainable relationships, social responsibility, authentic leadership, and problem-solving skills.

The future of the world quite literally depends on humanity accessing its Spiritual Intelligence. But the abolition of God, religion, and spirituality

from modern-secular culture, and the prioritization of knowledge over wisdom, has left us in a place of desperate spiritual poverty.

"No problem can be solved from the same consciousness that created it," was Albert Einstein's observation. We need a new spiritual consciousness. The material consciousness that got us into this mess will not get us out of it.

Politics, economics, and technology will always fail to address our greatest challenges, because they exist on the lower plane of material consciousness where the problems themselves were created. The solutions we desperately need can only be found on the higher spiritual plane of consciousness.

It is time to stop searching for worldly solutions to spiritual problems.

Should we participate vigorously in the political process? Absolutely, but with a clear understanding of its limitations. Should we courageously seek to bring a universal fairness to our laws? Absolutely, but let us never forget that laws are required where our humanity fails.

Our decency and humanity should ensure that children don't go to bed hungry, that the elderly have the care they need, that the sick are tended to, and that young people are educated.

Law is a poor substitute for love. Laws take over where our love runs short. Laws compel us to do what we should do willingly. Laws cannot legislate love and only love can take us from the current state of affairs to the world we all want to live in.

A government is no more capable of solving the most pressing issues of our times than it is of raising a child or healing a troubled marriage.

The role of a government is limited by the IQ, EQ, and SQ of the citizens that put that government in place, and by the virtue and character of the men and women who make up that government.

Our spiritual expansion, both personal and collective, is essential. Holy Moments facilitate that spiritual expansion and at the same time transform the world. When the Good Samaritan stopped to help, he did not simply bandage the stranger's wounds, he changed that man's whole world.

Holy Moments change the world. You may be inclined to reject this as idealistic, but if you will resist the temptation for just a few more pages, I believe I will prove to you that it is true.

Which of the world's problems would not be solved by Holy Moments? They may not be solved today, and it may take longer than we would prefer, but in the long run Holy Moments are the most effective way to sustainably solve our problems.

The world needs Good Samaritans. The world needs Holy Moments. It may be an ancient solution, but it is the solution that works. It has never been tried and found wanting.

The world is desperately in need of change. We are agreed on that. The real question is, what are *you* willing to do about it?

THE POWER OF HOLY MOMENTS

I have used the word flourish several times throughout this book. It means vigorous growth and development. The dictionary meaning is helpful, but like many things, we know it when we see it.

There is a plant here on my desk. Its broad leaves are green, rich with nutrients, and they glimmer in the sun. It is flourishing. I can tell just by looking at it. It is bursting with life. My children are in the yard playing. I can hear their squeals of delight and feel their energy as I sit here writing. They are bursting with life. They are flourishing.

Plants and children do it effortlessly. Their natural instincts lead them to flourish. We adults need to re-learn the art of flourishing. Holy Moments will teach us if we allow them to.

There is so much we have yet to learn about ourselves. The power you possess to create Holy Moments is a perfect example.

We have all heard phrases like ripple effect, domino effect, butterfly effect, snowball effect, and compounding effect. Each of these phenomena are astoundingly powerful, and yet, take them all, multiply them by infinity, and you will still have barely a glimpse of the power contained in each Holy Moment.

One day, when God invites us into His library to read His history books, we will see that it is so. On that day we will discover that seemingly insignificant acts, the smallest acts of kindness, unnoticed acts of generosity, set in motion a series of events that altered the whole course of human history.

The ripple effect begins with a single ripple, the domino effect with a single domino, and so on. But we have been seduced by the spectacular, so we dismiss small as insignificant. Holy Moments are usually small and simple. This is why we dismiss the idea that they could transform our lives and change the world. We have a bias against things that are simple, even though there is genius in simplicity. We have a bias against small, thinking that bigger is always better.

As a result, when life offers us a choice, these biases often lead us to make poor decisions. Let this example illustrate the point. Suppose someone offered you the choice between one million dollars today or a single penny that doubled every day for 31 days, which would you choose? Most people's minds go instantly toward the million dollars. But if you picked the penny that doubled every day for 31 days, you'd have over ten million dollars. $10,737,418.24 to be exact.

It's a fun illustration. But the consequences of this compounding effect when applied to Holy Moments are even more profound and far-reaching. So much so, that there is no place in the world, no situation in society, no part of our lives, that Holy Moments cannot reach and transform.

The Butterfly Effect suggests that every action, no matter how small, has an effect on the world around it. It is a scientific theory that has been explained with the idea that a butterfly flapping its wings in your neighborhood could cause a typhoon on the other side of the world.

Now, we know that a single act like a butterfly flapping its wings cannot directly cause a typhoon. Small acts can, however, be the catalyst that sets in motion a chain-reaction that leads to enormous outcomes.

This theory may seem abstract, but we experience the Butterfly Effect in human behavior all the time. Let's explore a practical example.

Bruce Dunn lost his wallet. A thirteen-year-old girl named Amanda found it and returned it. Bruce took two one-hundred-dollar bills from his wallet, and handed them to Amanda with the instructions, "Spend one on yourself and spend the other on someone else."

He didn't think much about it until four months later when someone sent him a picture they saw online. The people in the picture were holding up signs that said, "Thank you Bruce Dunn."

Bruce was stunned. It was a group of people in Honduras. Amanda had an assignment at school to study life in a poorer country and she had chosen Honduras. Around the time when Bruce gave her the money there had been a hurricane there, so Amanda picked a village on a map, and contacted a local church in that village. She told them the story and arranged to send the money. With $100 they were able to host a party for the whole village. The photo was the village saying thank you.

"What do you call that?" I asked Bruce when he told me the story. "I don't know," he said, "but I have done it a few times now and I am always amazed at what happens."

"I call that a Holy Moment grant," I said. He smiled. Since hearing his story I have made a couple of Holy Moment grants myself. Each one has a story and it's fun to watch them unfold.

Every Holy Moment increases the goodness and the goodwill in the world.

What is goodwill? Goodwill is a friendly, cooperative, and helpful attitude. Goodwill can make the whole difference in a relationship. A relationship guided by an attitude that is friendly, cooperative, and helpful, is radically different to a relationship tormented by the opposite. And the whole world is a collection of relationships. One relationship multiplying the next, one relationship compounding upon another.

You are walking through the grocery store, and someone smiles at you. A burst of joy goes through you, you smile back, and you begin to glow. Your response may even feel involuntary, and that's because it's so natural. We do it without reflection, instruction, or conscious thought, because it is who we are when we are at our best. The other person's smile tapped into the goodness and joy that was already within you.

Smiling at someone is a Holy Moment. Smiling is contagious. Holy Moments are contagious. Every Holy Moment inspires another one.

The Butterfly Effect of even the smallest Holy Moments are astounding.

Every collaboration with God yields unimaginable fruit. Moses liberated the Israelites in collaboration with God. Mary gave birth to Jesus by collaborating with God. The boy with five loaves and two fish fed thousands of people in collaboration with God.

You too can collaborate with God. And by collaborating with God to create one Holy Moment today, you never know who will be touched by the chain reaction you set off. It is impossible to predict where these Holy Moments will lead, but they will lead somewhere. Holy Moments never die. Every expression of goodness lives on forever. It finds a way to live on in other people, in other places, and in other times. This is how imperfect people collaborate with God to remake the world.

Here is a short fable that illustrates the point.

A British family went to Scotland one summer for a vacation. The mother and father were looking forward to enjoying the beautiful Scottish countryside with their son.

But one day the son wandered off all by himself and got into trouble. As he walked through the woods, he came across an abandoned swimming hole, and as most boys his age do, he took off his clothes and jumped in!

He was totally unprepared for what happened next. Before he had time to enjoy the pool of water, he was seized by a vicious attack of cramps. He began calling for help while fighting a losing battle with the cramps to stay afloat.

Fortunately, a farm boy was working in a nearby field. When he heard the frantic cries for help, he rescued the English boy and brought him to safety.

The father of the boy who had been rescued was of course very grateful. The next day, he went to meet the youth who had saved his son's life. As the two talked, the Englishman asked the brave lad what he planned to do with his future.

The boy answered, "I'll be a farmer like my father."

The grateful father said, "Is there something else you'd rather do?"

"Oh, yes!" answered the Scottish lad. "I've always wanted to be a doctor. But we are poor and could never afford to pay for the education."

"Never mind that," said the Englishman. "You shall have your heart's desire and study medicine. Make your plans, and I'll take care of the costs."

So, the Scottish lad did indeed become a doctor.

The legend of this fable says that years later, in

December of 1943, Winston Churchill (the English boy) became deathly ill with pneumonia while in North Africa. His life was saved for a second time by the Scottish boy (Sir Alexander Fleming). This time with a new drug Fleming had invented, the first antibiotic, penicillin. Two years later under the unshakable leadership of Churchill, Britain and her Allies would defeat Hitler and the Nazis, ending the most diabolical regime in history.

You never know how far your Holy Moments will reach.

GOD'S MATH LESSON

How many times have you thought about Holy Moments since you started reading this book? How many opportunities have you seized to create Holy Moments? How many Holy Moments have you witnessed?

There is something about the concept that is so powerful that simply becoming aware of it provides a new lens to see life through. It's invigorating, energizing, and hope-filled.

Still, if I asked you to go out and create a million Holy Moments you would feel overwhelmed. This feeling would probably lead you to conclude that it is impossible for you to create a million Holy Moments. But is it? That depends on whose math class you take.

Can we change the world? Most people believe it is impossible. They believe the culture has become too powerful and nothing we can do will alter that. I don't believe that, and this is why. It is called the principle of Spiritual Multiplication.

What is Spiritual Multiplication? It is a method that Jesus himself chose as the foundation of His ministry, and the strategy He put in place to change the world.

It is based on one very simple idea: Invest in a small group of people, teaching them how to create Holy Moments, then empower them to go out and do the same for another small group of people.

These are the two collaborations that will change the world: Collaborate with God to create Holy Moments, and collaborate with Him again to teach other people how to create Holy Moments.

How many people? Three. That's all it takes. Three people. If every person who read this book committed to teaching three other people to create Holy Moments, we would change the world.

My dream is to unleash a massive tidal wave of Holy Moments by raising up an amazing grassroots movement to transform our culture one Holy Moment at a time.

Your mission is to create Holy Moments in your own life and teach three other people about Holy Moments. Everything you need to do that is in this book.

It may seem like too little to have any real impact, it may seem like it would take forever at that rate, but not once you understand God's math lesson. Let's take a look at the divine strategy known as Spiritual Multiplication.

You are just one person: (1).

You teach three other people about Holy Moments: $1 + (1 \times 3 = 3) = 4$.

And those 3 new people each teach 3 other people: $4 + (3 \times 3 = 9) = 13$.

And those 9 new people each teach three more
13 + (9 x 3 = 27) = 40.

And so it goes...

40 + (27 x 3 = 81) = 121

121 + (81 x 3 = 243) = 364

364 + (243 x 3 = 729) = 1,093

1,093 + (729 x 3 = 2,187) = 3,280

3,280 + (2,187 x 3 = 6,561) = 9,841

9,841 + (6,561 x 3 = 19,683) = 29,524

29,524 + (19,683 x 3 = 59,049) = 88,573

88,573 + (59,049 x 3 = 177,147) = 265,720. That's the
whole city of Arlington, Virginia.

265,720 + (177,147 x 3 = 531,441) = 797,161

797,161 + (531,441 x 3 = 1,594,323) = 2,391,484.
That's more people than live in Philadelphia and Austin combined.

2,391,484 + (1,594,323 x 3 = 4,782,969) = 7,174,453

7,174,453 + (4,782,969 x 3 = 14,348,907) = 21,523,360.
That's more than the entire populations of New York,
Chicago, and Los Angeles.

21,523,360 + (14,348,907 x 3 = 43,046,721) =

64,570,081. There are 195 countries in the world, this is more than the population of 57 of those countries combined.

64,570,081+ (43,046,721 x 3 = 129,140,163) = 193,710,244.

193,710,244 + (129,140,163 x 3 = 387,420,489) = 581 million. That's almost twice the population of the United States. And that's just 18 cycles.

581,130,733 + (387,420,489 x 3 = 1,162,261,467) = 1.75 billion.

1,743,392,200 + (1,162,261,467 x 3=3,486,784,401) = 5.2 billion.

5,230,176,601 + (3,486,784,401x3=10,460,353,203) = 15.7 billion.

There are less than eight billion people on the planet today. It would take less than 21 cycles to reach the whole world's population. Just one more cycle and you would reach the entire population of the next 100 years. That's the power of Spiritual Multiplication.

The principle of Spiritual Multiplication is real, it's

powerful, and it demonstrates how people like you and me can change the world by collaborating with God.

This is the power of God's math. The world has problems, nobody disagrees with that. Holy Moments and Spiritual Multiplication are the answer.

It's time for us all to stop making excuses and to encourage each other to discover what is possible. It's your turn, and my turn. It's time to do our part—to renew our commitment to walking with God, to create Holy Moments, to become the-best-version-of-ourselves, and to pray for God to lead us to the three people He wants us to share the wisdom of Holy Moments with.

"I am only one person—what can I do?" This is a common excuse. Let's banish it from our hearts and minds. You can do your part. Can you change the world single-handedly? No. But don't let what you can't do interfere with what you can do. Do your part. That's all. Just do your part.

Do not let your part be left undone. That's how

the world got to be a mess. People like you and me let their small part in God's plan go undone. It is the compounding impact of people not doing their part that has led the world to be the mess it is today.

If everyone who read this book passed the wisdom of Holy Moments on to three people, the concept would spread around the world at a dizzying speed. There are more than one million pre-orders for this book. Let's look at God's math.

1 million + (1 million x 3 = 3 million) = 4 million.

4 million + (3 million x 3 = 9 million) = 13 million.

13 million + (9 million x 3 = 27 million) = 40 million.

40 million + (27 million x 3 = 81 million) = 121 million.

121 million + (81 million x 3 = 243million) = 364 million. The population of the United States today is 333 million people.

364 million + (243 million x 3 = 729 million) = 1 billion.

1,093,000,000 + (720,000,000 x 3 = 2,187,000,000) = 3.3 billion.

3,280,000,000 + (2,187,000,000 x 3 = 6,561,000,000) = 10 billion = Everyone. Everywhere.

Five cycles to share the wisdom of Holy Moments with every person in the United States of America. Eight cycles to share this wisdom with the whole world.

"Everyone who reads the book won't do it," someone said last week. I know that. But here's the beautiful thing. Lots of people won't stop once they share the wisdom of Holy Moments with three people. The joy they get from sharing it with three people will lead them to share it with three more people. When they see how it impacts those people, they will want to share it with everyone who crosses their path.

Don't forget to visit HolyMomentsBook.com and request six free copies of this book to give to the people you feel called to share this message with.

Let's turn our attention toward creating Holy Moments one at a time. It's true, you are just one person—but you are capable of collaborating with God to create thousands of helpful, hopeful, tender, loving

Holy Moments that will inspire other people to do the same. You are a Butterfly Effect unto yourself.

All this will unleash an unimaginable sense of meaning and purpose in your life. The kind of meaning and purpose many people spend their whole life searching for and never find.

So, begin today. Identify the three people you are going to share the wisdom of Holy Moments with. I think you will discover once you have shared this with three, you won't be able to stop. And for the first time in a long time, perhaps for the first time ever, your life will be dripping with meaning, and you will be making the contribution you always knew you could.

TWO CONVERSATIONS

I had two conversations recently that have been intertwining in my mind ever since. Someone made a passing comment, "Christianity is just too complicated." That same day someone asked me, "If you had to summarize how to live as a Christian in ten words or less, how would you do it?"

I've been thinking about that question ever since. The Christian life is quite simple in a sense. If I had to summarize it in ten words, I would say: You were made in the image of God. Act accordingly!

Made in the image of God, you have an astounding capacity for goodness. The reservoir of goodness within you is vast. Will you hoard it or share it? When you share this goodness with others, the reservoir within you is supernaturally replenished. It is a never-ending source.

Now is your time. Time to be bold with your goodness. Time to start creating Holy Moments.

You were made in the image of God. Act accordingly!

part four

The Power of One Idea

POSSIBILITIES

Everybody said it couldn't be done.

It was simply impossible for a human being to run a mile in under 4 minutes the experts proclaimed with arrogant certainty. The debate reached fever-pitch in the running community in the 1940s as Gunder Hagg of Sweden ran a mile in 4:06, then 4:04, and then 4:01. But the 40s came and went without anyone breaking the 4-minute barrier.

Gunder Hagg's record sat untouched for nine long years, running experts grew even more confident in their assertion. They believed the human body had reached its limits, but one man visualized breaking the barrier.

Roger Banister believed it was possible.

In 1954, while practicing medicine and studying for an advanced degree at Oxford, Banister ran the mile in 3:59.4. It was a seminal moment in the world of sports and Roger Banister instantly became a legend.

His record lasted just 46 days. Ten years later, high school students were breaking the 4-minute mile, and the world record today is 3:43.13. Since Banister broke the elusive 4-minute barrier more than 2,000 people have run sub-four-minute miles in competition. What was once considered impossible is now routine.

We have explored the reach of the human mind and the human body. Now it is time to explore the reach of the soul.

The human spirit has not reached its limits. Not even close.

Holy Moments may have once seemed impossible, but they are not. It's time to make Holy Moments routine.

Human beings are capable of incredible things.

You are capable of incredible things. Most people live and die without even scratching the surface of their potential. You may have explored your physical and intellectual limits, but have you ever really tried to explore your spiritual capacity? Until we do, we have no idea what we are actually capable of.

It is time to explore your soul-potential.

THE POWER OF ONE IDEA

Some ideas are so powerful that simply becoming aware of them changes our lives forever. Holy Moments is such an idea.

Once you hear about Holy Moments, the idea is impossible to forget. You cannot unhear it. It creates an immediate paradigm shift. Everywhere you go you will see opportunities to participate in Holy Moments, you will see other people collaborating with God to create Holy Moments, and you will witness possible Holy Moments being squandered. You will see Holy Moments for the rest of your life, whether you do something about them or not.

Sometimes you will accept the invitation to collaborate with God in a Holy Moment, and sometimes your laziness, procrastination, or selfishness will get the better of you. Either way, you will begin to notice how you feel in each case, and you will observe the ripple effects—positive or negative—that result from your choices.

We live in a world drowning in information and desperate for wisdom. The piercing clarity of Holy Moments brings wisdom and clarity to our lives. The power of this one idea, shines the bright light of possibility on each moment.

The idea itself, like an ice-cold glass of water on the hottest day of summer, is refreshingly practical. The principle of Holy Moments is not just a theory, it is eminently practical. The moment you first heard about it, you immediately started seeing possibilities for Holy Moments all around you. And the idea is so simple and practical that it allows you to immediately start having an impact with your life in profound and meaningful ways.

This soul-expanding concept is a breath of fresh air in a world polluted by so many soul-diminishing ideas and experiences.

So, let me ask you: What's the most powerful thing in your life right now? This idea. At this very moment, this idea of Holy Moments is the most powerful thing in your life. And as Victor Hugo observed, "Nothing is more powerful than an idea whose time has come."

Now you have a decision to make. This idea is im-mensely powerful. Will you embrace it or reject it? Dabble with it or passionately deploy it in your life? Will you allow the Holy Moments concept to release your soul-potential?

I sometimes wonder what the difference is be-tween a person who reads one of my books and has a life-changing experience, and a reader who doesn't. For some people this book will be a defining moment in their lives. For others it will be just another book. It's the same book for both readers. So, I have to con-clude, there is something special happening inside the reader whose life changes.

The choice is yours.

This is the idea. You are the person. Now is the time.

A WORLD FULL OF DISTRACTION

All parents have phrases they use over and over. When I am trying to get my children's attention, especially in a situation that involves safety, I find myself saying, "Focus." There is something about the use of a single word and the word itself that calls them to attention.

It seems we all need to heed the warning to focus from time to time. Our lives have been overrun by distractions, and these distractions are preventing us from experiencing life to the fullest.

It's time to move from distraction to focus. Living a less distracted life is the path to peace and happiness. But it is impossible to simply say we will ignore the siren call of the myriad distractions that stalk us day and night. We need something to focus on if we are to ignore their constant and seductive beckoning.

Distractions are the siren call of the culture. The

origins of the siren call can be found in Greek mythology. Sirens were creatures, half bird and half woman, who lured sailors to their destruction with the sweetness of their songs.

There may be more distractions than ever before, but distractions have always presented danger for humanity. Homer wrote about this in his epic tale *The Odyssey* eight centuries before the birth of Jesus.

Odysseus was one of the most influential Greek heroes of the Trojan War. *The Odyssey* is the story of his quest to return home after the war.

The goddess Circe advised Odysseus that the Sirens sat in a meadow filled with rotting bodies, waiting for ships to come by. They would sing irresistible songs to lure men to their doom. Sailors would steer their boats closer to shore to hear the melodies and would end up crashing their boats on the rocks.

Circe told Odysseus to plug his men's ears with wax, so they would not be tempted to steer their ships off course in the direction of the Sirens. Odysseus further ordered his sailors to tie him to the mast, and to leave him there until danger had past, no matter how much he begged them to release him.

Are you living a life of focus or distraction? What distractions have taken your life off course? What distractions are trying to lure you to your doom? Do you believe a life of focus would be more fulfilling than a life of distraction?

Like Odysseus we all need Circe's warning.

Odysseus plugged his ears and had himself tied to the mast. What will you do to save yourself from distraction in your own odyssey?

Distractions can be alluring and seductive. They can be entertaining for a time, but a life that bounds from one distraction to another will inevitably become an empty and meaningless life. This tragedy is all too common. Don't let that be your story.

It's not too late to chart a new course. It's not too late to set aside all the trivial distractions and bring meaningful focus to your life. Allow the principle of Holy Moments to guide you in each moment from this day on, and you will soon find yourself sailing toward the most beautiful sunset of your life with the wind at your back.

Émile Coué, the French psychologist, is famous for the mantra, "Every day, in every way, I'm getting better and better." I had a teacher as a child who encouraged us to repeat it to ourselves when we were struggling academically or athletically.

Many people look down on such techniques, and yet it is breathtaking how powerful they can be in our lives. The mind is a powerful tool.

I am reimagining it now: Every day, in every way, I'm creating more and more Holy Moments.

Say it to yourself over and over. Use it to focus. Train your heart, mind, and soul to seek out opportunities to collaborate with God and create Holy Moments everywhere you go.

NEVER STAY DISCOURAGED

"Never get discouraged," I used to say. But then I realized that we all do get discouraged from time to time, and that's okay. For whatever reason it is part of the journey.

Now, when I meet people who are trying to do good in this world, I always leave them with these words, "Never stay discouraged. You will get discouraged, that's life, part of humanity, comes with the territory of trying to do good in this world. But people desperately need what you are doing, so never stay discouraged for long."

I was nineteen years old when I started speaking and writing. How it all happened is baffling to me as I look back now. I grew up in Australia and before my first trip to Europe, my spiritual mentor took me aside one day and said, "Promise me you will never forget what I am about to tell you. You will only ever see less than one percent of the impact you have on people's lives. Reflect on that whenever you get discouraged."

The reason I am sharing this with you now is because I get discouraged myself at times, and I know you will get discouraged at times too. My own discouragement has taught me never to miss an opportunity to encourage others.

In your quest to fill your life with Holy Moments you will encounter skeptics, cynics, critics, people who hate you for no good reason. Others will gossip about you, and some will maliciously attack you in ways you never imagined. I know because this has happened to me, and I have witnessed it happen to many others. I am telling you because I don't want you to be blindsided by it.

Just keep in mind that there has always been a battle between good and evil in this world. Best to put yourself on the right side of that battle. But even when things seem dark, even when you are discouraged, don't let discouragement possess you. Find a way to exorcise your discouragement daily.

I have found that discouragement is a devil that needs to be driven from our lives with inspiration. I need a daily dose of inspiration: books, movies, music, quotes, friends, family, history, prayer, reflection, meditation, and laughter, always laughter. Find the inspiration you need and drink from those waters each day.

You will get discouraged, just don't stay discouraged. Rest if you need to rest, take a break by all means, seek inspiration, remember you are not in this alone, and then, press on!

Decide here and now, today, that you will do your little part to bring more Holy Moments to this world. Say to yourself over and again, "I will not leave my part undone."

Persevere when people criticize you. Persevere when the demons of your past try to lure you back to their darkness. Persevere when your inner critic tries to make you feel like you are unworthy. We all need what we don't deserve, and God is glad to give it to us.

You may be able to do very little, that's okay, persist in doing the little you can do. There is great satisfaction in persistence. It's hard to describe. But after doing something worthwhile for many years, persisting at it no matter what, you experience a delightful pleasure just at the knowing that you have persisted through good times and bad.

Nothing significant can be accomplished without perseverance. "Nothing in this world can take the place of persistence. Talent will not; nothing is more common than unsuccessful men with talent. Genius will not; unrewarded genius is almost a proverb. Education will not; the world is full of educated derelicts. Persistence and determination alone are omnipotent. The slogan 'Press On!' has solved and always will solve the problems of the human race," was Calvin Coolidge's observation.

So, press on! One Holy Moment at a time.

BE BOLD

What are you going to do with the rest of your life? I know, I asked you already, earlier, but you have had more time to consider things now.

We are all confronted, sooner or later, with two of life's quintessential questions: Are you satisfied with your life? Are you satisfied with the direction the world is moving in?

The mere fact that the questions are emerging is

usually a solid indication that we are dissatisfied with both to some degree. It's time to listen to that dissatisfaction. Don't swat it aside like an annoying fly. Go deep into your dissatisfaction. It is a profound messenger that comes to reveal your future.

"Be bold and mighty forces will come to your aid," was Goethe's observation. Boldness is a beautiful thing. When we see boldness alive in another person it is incredibly attractive. There is power in boldness. The power to explore new possibilities and the power to get unstuck.

It is time to move beyond our timidity and boldly participate in each moment of life.

Boldness requires a single clear priority. Boldness is single-minded. You cannot boldly pursue many things, that's recklessness, and the two should never be confused.

Too often we are bold when we should be timid, and timid when we should be bold.

Holy Moments require boldness.

The world needs a massive outpouring of

goodness. It needs the healing tonic of goodness that Holy Moments release. But the culture is so resistant to goodness, so in order to unleash the tidal wave of goodness needed to heal the culture, we need to be bold.

When you are afraid, build confidence and momentum one small Holy Moment at a time. You can do small things boldly, and boldness is compatible with patience. Momentum will build fast enough. And once your efforts to create Holy Moments gathers a little momentum, it will look bold and unstoppable to others, but you will know that it was small and fragile when it began.

"Be bold and mighty forces will come to your aid." It's time to awaken the greatness of the human spirit within you. And nothing will awaken the greatness God has placed within you like Holy Moments.

You were made in the image of God. Act accordingly!

Jesus told a parable that has been a guiding star for me over the past 30 years. The parable is about a farmer who goes out to sow seeds in his field. He sows his seed boldly and generously.

Some of the seed falls on the path, some falls in the shallow rocky soil, some falls among the thorns, but some of the seed falls in the richest soil and produces a bountiful harvest. The harvest is thirty, sixty, and one hundred times what was sown.

Holy Moments have those kinds of returns.

The danger is to overthink and complicate our efforts. For a long time, I thought the different types of soil were different people. But over time, I have grown in awareness and become less judgmental. The truth is most people's hearts have a little bit of each type of soil. We each have the capacity for great good and for great evil. We get to choose.

When I look back on my life, I see that so many people generously sowed goodness into my heart. They filled my life with Holy Moments. Many of them probably thought they had wasted their time on me, but here I am, and I would not be here today, if not for their generosity. I am part of their Butterfly Effect, though most of them are unaware of it. You are ben-efiting from their Holy Moments also, even though you will never meet or know them.

There are many critics in my life. I never imag-ined you could have so many critics in an effort to do good. I was naïve. And I do get discouraged. But by some grace I have learned to find inspiration every-where I go.

Besides, consider the other options. Should I give into the cynics, skeptics, and critics, and the selfish-ness, hopelessness, and hatred they spread every-where they go?

I will not. Every age has tyrants and each of us has to decide to face them or cower to them. Meaning-lessness and hopelessness are two of the tyrants that torment the people of this age. They perpetuate the madness that has gripped so many people. They may seem overwhelming, even invincible, but I will not lose hope for I know they are not.

My reasons are very simple. Each Holy Moment offers someone a path out of the madness and demonstrates the beauty of what is possible. Holy Moments have the power to bring the tyrannies of meaninglessness and hopelessness to an end. Holy Moments hold the power to set people free from meaninglessness and hopelessness to live rich and purpose-filled lives. Critics are quickly forgotten. And I simply refuse to underestimate God.

So, what am I going to do?

I will press on. I'm going to keep sowing Holy Moments in my own imperfect way, everywhere I go, with every person I meet, every chance I get, reminding myself daily that the Messiah is indeed among us!

The critics will say "but so much of the seed doesn't fall on rich ground." They are right, but they are missing the point, because you never know whose heart the next handful of seeds will fall into. And you never know what that person will go on to do with his/her life. So, I am going to keep sowing, generously.

The last question is: What are you going to do?

If you would allow me to make a recommendation: Do your part! Start sowing Holy Moments everywhere you go. Join me. Join others. Become part of a grassroots movement that is changing lives and transforming the world one Holy Moment at a time.

Do what you can, where you are, with what you've got... and trust that others, hundreds of them, thousands of them, in every town, suburb, village, and city across these United States (and around the world) will do what they can also. And together we will unleash such a force of goodness that people will marvel and wonder how it happened.

Your Holy Moments can have an enormous impact.

So, do your part! When people do their part miracles happen. I have seen these miracles. An astounding ripple effect is set in motion when people simply decide once and for all to do their part.

This Holy Moments movement that is emerging is a perfect example. "How did all this happen?" people will ask. "It's a miracle," others will say. They will be right. But it's a very specific type of miracle. It's the type of miracle that is guaranteed to happen when a bunch of people get together, decide enough is enough, and commit to doing their part.

So, decide today, once and for all, that each day for the rest of your life will have a positive impact. Decide to be the difference that makes the difference. Decide, that your part, however small, will not be left undone. Decide to light a candle rather than curse the darkness. Decide to collaborate with God to create Holy Moments. And decide to share the wisdom of Holy Moments as far and wide as possible.

And do it boldly.

I hope you enjoyed

holy moments

It is a privilege to write for you.
I hope it nourished you
in the ways you needed to be fed
at this time in your life.

Matthew Kelly

About the Author

MATTHEW KELLY is a bestselling author, speaker, thought leader, entrepreneur, consultant, spiritual leader, and innovator.

He has dedicated his life to helping people and organizations become the-best-version-of-themselves. Born in Sydney, Australia, he began speaking and writing in his late teens while he was attending business school. Since that time, 5 million people have attended his seminars and presentations in more than 50 countries.

Today, Kelly is an internationally acclaimed speaker, author, and business consultant. His books have been published in more than 30 languages, have appeared on the *New York Times*, *Wall Street Journal*, and *USA Today* bestseller lists, and have sold more than 50 million copies.

In his early-twenties he developed "the-best-version-of-yourself" concept and has been sharing it in every arena of life for more than twenty-five years. It is quoted by presidents and celebrities, athletes and their coaches, business leaders and innovators. Though perhaps it is never more powerfully quoted than when a mother or father asks a child, "Will that help you become the-best-version-of-yourself?"

Kelly's personal interests include golf, music, art, literature, investing, spirituality, and spending time with his wife, Meggie, and their children Walter, Isabel, Harry, Ralph, and Simon.

Subscribe to
Matthew's YouTube Channel!

 YouTube

www.youtube.com/matthewkellyauthor

Visit **MatthewKelly.com** for his Blog
and so much more.